Bears

Emma Helbrough

Designed by Michelle Lawrence
and Josephine Thompson

Illustrated by Tetsuo Kushii and Adam Larkum
Bear consultant: Dr. Lynn Rogers, Wildlife Research Institute
Reading consultant: Alison Kelly, Roehampton University

Contents

Hairy bears

Bears are big, furry animals. They have large, round heads with small eyes and ears.

These bears are brown bears.

Young cubs

Baby bears are called cubs. They are born in winter in small caves or hollow trees.

Cubs get food by drinking their mother's rich milk.

Mother bears comfort their cubs when they're afraid.

Mother bears lick their cubs to keep them clean.

Cubs spend most of the time in their den sleeping and drinking milk.

Snowy dens

Polar bear cubs are born in winter too.

Female polar
bears dig dens in
the snow.

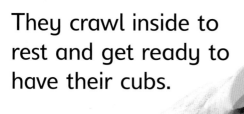

They crawl inside to
rest and get ready to
have their cubs.

Their cubs are
born inside the
snow den.

This polar bear cub is sitting outside
its den. The cub has thick fur that
helps to keep it warm.

Polar bear cubs' fur is very white.
It turns creamy as the cubs grow older.

Growing up

In the spring, cubs leave the den with their mother.

Cubs spend a lot of time exploring, but they stay close to their mother.

Brown bear cubs leave their mother when they are about three years old.

Mother bears usually have one or two cubs at a time, but sometimes they have three.

A mother bear takes care of her cubs.

The mother leads her cubs to where they can find food.

If she needs to move a cub, she picks it up with her mouth.

Furry coats

All bears are covered in thick fur.

Polar bears live in icy places. Their fur is extra thick to keep them warm.

If a polar bear is too hot, it rubs its tummy in the snow to cool down.

Spectacled bears have white fur around their eyes which looks like a pair of glasses.

Sloth bears have long, shaggy fur. Their cubs travel on their mother's back.

The cubs grab a chunk of her fur with their front paws.

They scramble up and hold on tight. Then she stands up.

Paws and claws

Bears' hands and feet are called paws.
On each paw there are five long claws.

Bears turn over rocks with their paws to look for insects to eat.

Some bears use their claws like a comb to keep their fur clean and neat.

Brown bears use
their claws to dig
up roots to eat.

Polar bears' paws
have grips, so they
don't slip on the ice.

Pandas have an extra bone in each paw.
They use it to grip bamboo plants to eat.

Lunchtime

Most bears eat many different foods, such as plants, fruit, nuts and insects.

Brown bears live on grasslands where there are lots of green plants to eat.

A sun bear knocks a wasps' nest out of a tree with its paws.

It uses its long claws to break into the wasps' nest.

Then, it licks up the grubs inside with its long tongue.

Bears often have bad teeth because they also eat honey and other sweet foods.

Some bears eat thousands of caterpillars in a day.

Sneaky hunters

Bears that eat meat have to catch their prey.

Brown bears pounce on small animals, such as squirrels and mice. They will even jump into water to hunt for food.

Polar bears hunt
seal pups which
live in tunnels
under the ice.

They thump the
ice with their front
paws to break
into a tunnel.

Polar bears catch adult seals too.

A polar bear
waits by a
hole in the ice.

A seal swims
up to the
hole for air.

The bear drags
the seal out
of the water.

Fishing fun

Bears that live near rivers go fishing.
They catch and eat huge salmon.

Brown bears stand at the
top of waterfalls, waiting
for fish to jump up.

As the fish jump, the
bears try to catch one
in their mouths.

When a bear catches
a fish, it carries it to
the riverbank to eat.

Brown bears usually catch about
15 salmon in a day.

Climbing trees

Bears often live in forests and most bears can climb trees.

A cub digs its claws into a tree trunk.

It grips the trunk with its back paws

Then it pulls itself up with its front paws.

Bears often sleep in trees. They feel safe high up in the air.

Cubs climb
trees when they
are afraid.

Sun bears bend
back tree branches
so they can lie
on them.

21

Standing up

Bears can stand on their two back legs.
They use their front paws to balance.

Some bears stand
up to eat fruit from
high tree branches.

Bears often stand up
to look around when
they hear a noise.

Polar bears stand up
to wrestle, but they
are only playing.

If a polar bear stood up in a house,
it would hit its head on the ceiling.

This bear is standing up to rub its back on a tree. It's rubbing a smell from its back onto the trunk.

Bears sniff trees to tell if other bears have been there.

23

Super swimmers

Polar bears are very good swimmers.
They can swim for hours without stopping.

They can jump
into the water.

A polar bear
climbs out of
the water onto
the ice.

It shakes
itself like a
wet dog to
dry off.

Then it rolls on
snow to soak
up the rest of
the water.

Polar bears paddle with
their front paws and steer
with their back paws.

Polar bears can hold their
breath underwater for two minutes.

Hot and cold

Bears live in many different places. Some live in hot forests and others live high up in cold mountains.

Some brown bears live near the sea.

They use their long claws to dig for shellfish to eat on beaches.

In hot summers, black bears lie in water to cool off.

Spectacled bears live in rainforests.

In the daytime, it's very, very hot, so the bears just sleep.

At night, when it's cooler, they wake up and search for food.

Playtime

Cubs are very playful, but adult bears play too.

Pandas swing on tree branches. They sometimes hang upside down from trees.

| Pandas climb up steep slopes. | They roll down to the bottom. | Then they climb back up again. |

Bears often lie on their backs and play with sticks and stones.

Glossary of bear words

Here are some of the words in this book you might not know. This page tells you what they mean.

 cub - a baby bear. Bears usually have one or two cubs at a time.

 den - the place where cubs are born and live when they are very young.

 fur - the fluffy hair all over a bear's body that keeps it warm.

 paws - a bear's hands and feet. Bears walk on all four paws.

 claws - spikes on bears' paws, which they use for digging and climbing.

 prey - an animal that a bear has caught to eat, such as a seal.

Websites to visit

You can visit exciting websites to find out more about bears.

To visit these websites, go to the Usborne Quicklinks website at **www.usborne.com/quicklinks**
Read the internet safety guidelines, and then type the keywords "**beginners bears**".

The websites are regularly reviewed and the links in Usborne Quicklinks are updated. However, Usborne Publishing is not responsible, and does not accept liability, for the content or availability of any website other than its own. We recommend that children are supervised while on the internet.

This mother polar bear is protecting her cub from the cold. Her body warms the cub, and her legs shield it from the icy wind.

Index

Acknowledgements

Photo credits

The publishers are grateful to the following for permission to reproduce material:
cover © Dan Guravich/CORBIS; p1 © Lisa & Mike Husar/Team Hussar Wildlife Photography; p2-3 © Paul A. Souders/CORBIS; p4 © Keren Su/CORBIS; p5 © Lynn and Donna Rogers/bearstudy.org; p7 © Mark Newman/FLPA; p8 © Eastcot Momatiuk/Getty Images; p9 © Mark Newman/Prisma Bildagentur AG/Alamy; p10 © Tui de Roy/photolibrary.com; p11 © Tui De Roy/Minden Pictures/FLPA; p12 © Tom and Pat Leeson/Leeson photos; p13 © Lisa & Mike Husar/Team Hussar Wildlife Photography; p14 © Bauer/Powerstock; p16 © Lynn and Donna Rogers/bearstudy.org; p17 © Andy Rouse/NHPA/Photoshot; p19 © Paul A. Souders/CORBIS; p20 © Gary W. Carter/CORBIS; p21 © Daniel J. Cox/photolibrary.com; p23 © Giel/Getty Images; p24 © Dr. Hinrich Bäsemann; p25 © Linda S. Milks/Toledo Zoo; p26-27 © Lynn and Donna Rogers/bearstudy.org; p28 © Lisa & Mike Husar/Team Hussar Wildlife Photography; p29 © Daniel J. Cox/photolibrary.com; p31 © Wayne R. Bilenduke/Getty Images. With thanks to Andi Norman and the North American Bear Center.